Dianna

Did You Know That He Doesn't Think Like You

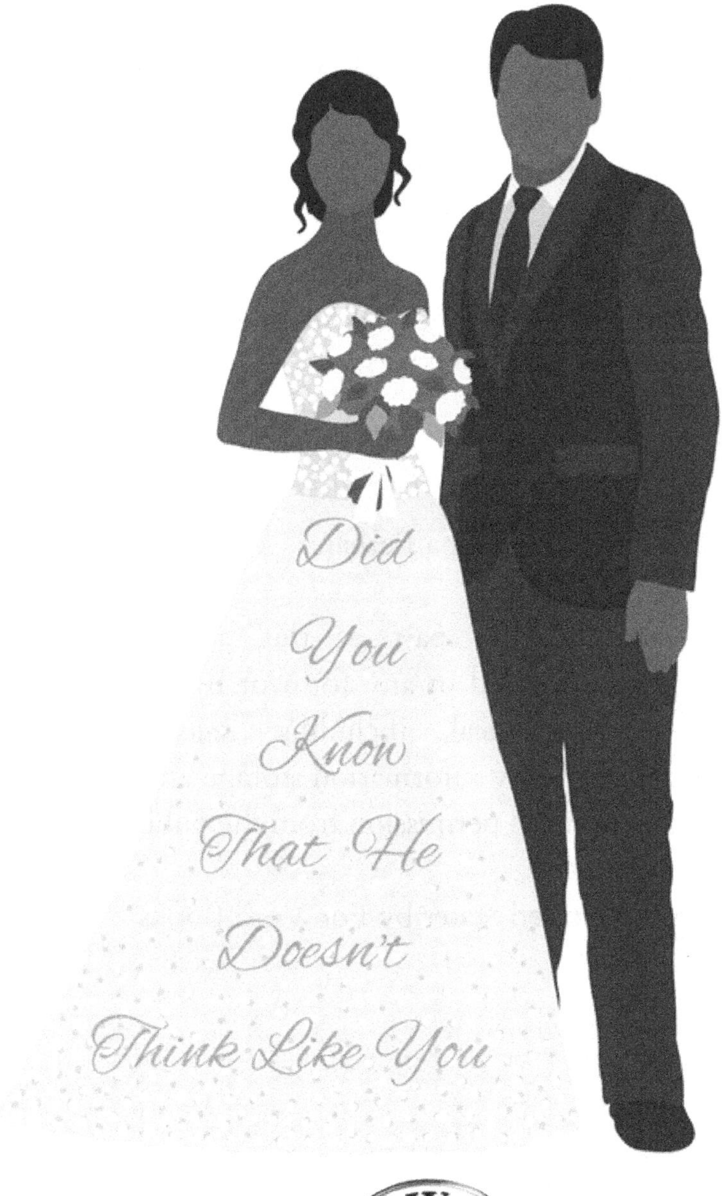

Did You Know That He Doesn't Think Like You
Published by ForWord Books
21143 Hawthorne Blvd, Ste 184
Torrance, CA 90503

Scripture quotations are taken or paraphrased from the following versions: King James Version, The Holy Bible.

ISBN 979-8-9882642-2-4

Copyright © 2023 by Dianna Bethany

All rights reserved. No part of this book may be reproduced or transmitted in any form or by any means, electronic or mechanical, including recording and photocopying, or by any information storage and retrieval system, without written permission from the publisher.

Published in the United States by ForWord Books

DEDICATION

I dedicate this writing to my head, James Bethany. You have shielded me from many storms, protected me from many hurts, and loved me through many faults. I am honored that you wanted to share your life, your dreams, and your goals with one such as I. May God continue to bless you and keep you with health, long life, prosperity, and more importantly, with me!!!!

Forever James and Dianna Bethany!

I dedicate this to women of all kinds; single; engaged; married; divorced; widowed; and those who are thinking about it! We can do it. With the help of God, we can do it! I pray that this writing helps and encourages you to continue to be strong and take your life to its next level, whatever that may be. Thank you for the time taken to even read this book! I am honored! Be Blessed.

Evangelist Dianna Bethany
"Lost But Not Forgotten Ministries"

FOREWORD

Marriage is honorable in all, (Hebrews 13:4a). Ever since the divine union of Adam and Eve, the institution of marriage has been between a man and a woman. Sometimes I am led to believe that men do not have a clue what women are all about. And we as women do not have a clue what men are all about.

It is so important to search the Scriptures on what Jesus has to say about marriage and follow His instructions. This book has very good instructions according to what scriptures to follow. Experience is the best teacher in any marriage. You must work at it as friends, lovers, and then as a team. You must learn to be single, single with Jesus Christ first, and then you can learn to love your mate the way the Bible says.

Man is not supposed to think like you. Philippians 2:5 states, "Let this mind be in you, which was also in Christ Jesus." "Husbands, love your wives, even as Christ also loved the church, and gave himself for it;" (Ephesians 5:25) For we are workmanship of Christ, created in Jesus Christ unto good works, which God hath before ordained that we should walk in them. (Ephesians 2:10) If we obey and walk in the Word of God, we can have a marriage made of God. In this book I see problems and I also see solutions that experiences have taught them to work it out together. Marriage is not a 50%/50% union but both should do 100%.

Evangelist Dianna Bethany has done an excellent job putting this book together. I do believe this is a good book. Congratulations and God bless you in your endeavors.

Evangelist, Dr. Sandra Price
1st Lady of Zion Temple Church of God In Christ - St. Louis, Missouri

PREFACE

What does marriage look like?

Is there a standard?

Where is the manual of the perfect marriage located and how can it be purchased?

All great questions, unfortunately, are questions that will forever be left unanswered for many. Whether you are already seasoned in the journey of marriage, or just desiring to be a spouse, there is one important factor that must be realized; you both have different thought processes.

The book, "Did You Know That He Doesn't Think Like You," takes the reader down the roads called, compromise, compassion, and understanding. It will identify what God says about marriage, how God defines the spousal role in marriage, and what the strength of unity concerning married couples looks like when we put God first.

My prayer is that this journal encourages you and brings to the forefront a more profound glimpse at how God sees marriage and our responsibility. Remember, WE CAN DO IT!

ACKNOWLEDGMENTS

My Lord and Savior Jesus Christ for the vision and for using me as the writing vessel for this manuscript.

My husband, James (my rock, my hero). Babe, you have ALWAYS been my biggest cheerleader! Always by my side! You're my ALWAYS! You're my FOREVER! I do not have adequate words to explain how I feel, so I'll just keep loving you and letting my love speak for me concerning you.

My children, David and Justin. You guys ARE my reason...for EVERYTHING! I do what I do and push like I do to show you that you can do ANYTHING you set your heart and mind to do. Don't give up on your dream! I love you both!!!!!!

My parents, Dad, John (still living and kicking!); father-in-love, the late James E Bethany Jr.; mother, the late Eva Dyson, and mother-in-love, the late Brenda Bethany. They birthed me, what else can I say? Without God and them, there is no me.

My brothers, the late Larry Thomas, the late Steven Thomas, and Bryan. Family is important to me and having you all in my life has been an adventure.

My sister-in-love, Angela. Thanks, sis, for all the talks and encouragement. I always wanted a sister and I'm grateful God gave me you.

My godmother, Dr. Evangelist Sandra Price. Mom, you have prayed for me through so much. You have seen the majority of my ups and downs. You never judged me or put me to the side. I will be your Snookum's forever!

My spiritual parents, Pastor Anthony and Dr. Momma Brannon. Mom and Dad, you have shown me how to walk in my calling. You have shown me how to remain integral and you continue to love me to a place of healing. You have pushed me to minister when I didn't feel adequate enough. I don't tell you everything, but somehow, you KNOW everything about me. Thank you, Mom and Dad!

My pastoral and spiritual leader support, Pastor Earl E. Nance, Sr. and Jr, Pastor Henry Price, the late Pastor Michael Fowler, the late Bishop RJ Ward, Bishop William Scott, Lady Dannette Fishburne Scott, the late Pastor Nathaniel Cole, Apostle Annie Cole, Pastor Tina Cole Evans, Pastor Anthony Brannon, Dr. Momma Brannon, Pastor Quentin Rudison, Lady Corrine Rudison, Bishop James L'Keith Jones, Lady Rosalind Jones, Bishop David C. Cooper, Co-Pastor Dr. Nina Cooper, Pastor Eddie McCall, Dr. Sharon McCall, and Pastor Karissa McCall. Thank you for loving me, teaching me, chastising me, lifting me, praying for me, pushing me, encouraging me, being real with me, listening to me, and allowing me to be. I stand on some great shoulders.

My Mentor, Pastor Toya Woods. YOU are amazing! What was once just thoughts in my mind to finish one day has now become my reality. I owe this to you Lady Woods! Everyone should have a Toya Woods in their lives. Thank you for praying for me, listening to me, pushing me, chastising me, and not condemning me when I knew I was not in place. I love you!

My publishers, Larry, Paris, and Langston Rodgers, and ForWord Books Publishing Family. I appreciate you all believing in what God has given me. I took a leap of faith and so did you! Thanks be unto God that He used you all to push me to my next level!

Finally, to EVERY person who has stood with me, helped me, encouraged me, pushed me, made me laugh, made me angry, made me cry, wiped my tears, and hugged me. If I named all of you, it would take up the ENTIRE book! Just know you have a special place in my heart, and I am eternally GRATEFUL for you all!!!

With Love,
Dianna Bethany

CONTENTS

Introduction
x

Chapter One
What Does God Say About Marriage?
1

Chapter Two
Independency versus Individuality
3

Chapter Three
He's Always A-HEAD of You
8

Chapter Four
At What Point Do We Become One?
12

Chapter Five
Where Do We Go From Here?
15

In Conclusion...
17

INTRODUCTION

In the year 2010, the divorce rate according to DivorceRate.com seemed as such:

Age	Women	Men
- Under 20 years old	27.6%	11.7%
- 20 to 24 years old	36.6%	38.8%
- 25 to 29 years old	16.4%	22.3%
- 30 to 34 years old	8.5%	11.6%
- 35 to 39 years old	5.1%	6.5%

The statistics also show that the divorce rate was at 50% during the year 2010. Meaning if 100 marry-50 divorce; if 50 marry-25 divorce; if 20 marry-10 divorce, if 2 marry-1 divorce. Wow!

In various faith groups, it is as follows according to Religioustolerance.org:

Denomination (in order of decreasing divorce rate) % who have been divorced:
- Non-denominational 34%
- Baptists 29%
- Mainline Protestants 25%
- Mormons 24%
- Catholics 21%
- Lutherans 21%

But no matter how you break it down, whether it be by race, age, gender, or denomination, this is still too high. Marriage is an honorable thing. It was never in the perfect will of God to have divorces, it was tolerated. Moses had to make the certificate of divorcement for legal purposes only, not because that is what God wanted. "They say unto him, Why did Moses then command to give a writing of divorcement, and to put her away? He saith unto them, Moses because of the hardness of your hearts suffered you to put away your wives: but from the beginning it was not so." (Matthew 19:7-8)

The covenant of marriage should remain a promise unbroken. For this promise is not only to your spouse, but it is to the Lord as well. What if God broke His covenant with us just because He was tired, or things didn't go the way He wanted, our lack of financial support, or our disobedience? Where would we be? I pray that this book will give you the opportunity to rethink before you walk away. Speak life into your marriage and fight for what God has ordained in your life. For what God has for you, it is for you.

CHAPTER ONE
What Does God Say About Marriage?

"Marriage is honourable in all, and the bed undefiled: but whoremongers and adulterers God will judge." (Hebrews 13:4)

"For the husband is the head of the wife, even as Christ is the head of the church: and he is the savior of the body." (Ephesians 5:23)

"Husbands, love your wives, even as Christ also loved the church, and gave himself for it;" (Ephesians 5:25)

Besides the fact that Webster's Dictionary defines marriage as "the state of being united to a person of the opposite sex as husband or wife in a consensual and contractual relationship recognized by law;" marriage is an honorable union between a man and a woman. God uses this union as a model of Christ and the church. When one leaves his or her parent(s) and cleaves to their spouse, it's not a bad thing at all. It's the door opener for you to have children and become a family. But like all things that are to become mature, it takes work, time, and a heart to help make it last. The adversary hates the fact that marriage is another form of a covenant between God and His love for His people; so therefore his (satan's) mission is to destroy and annihilate anything of unity. His main tools are the lack of communication, the loss of understanding, and the disappearance of love.

We as women tend to forget that God made man the HEAD; the LEADER. As women, we long for our independency. Having our own things, acquiring our heart desires, and gaining prominent careers are all so important to us. Then the time comes when our loving being wants to share all of our accomplishments with someone else, a male counterpart, then eventually with our children. Sharing doesn't mean to gain loss of, right? So, what happened? Why do we feel like our independent nature is gone? Why do we feel like we are under such a pressure squeeze with the partaking of a new regime of life? Oh yeah, it's that word "submissive." OH MY GOD!!!! I am no longer myself. WHY, WHY? Well, before you lose yourself, let's dig deeper into this life of yours, shall we?

CHAPTER TWO
Independency versus Individuality

First of all, know that you are an individual, not an independ-ual. Independency is a part of one's individuality; it's just an attribute. Everyone who is born is of one body, one heart, one soul, one mind, and one will. But even with those qualities of one, it's up to you to use them on your own.

So why have we become so fearful of being submissive? Submission is an offering; it's our sacrifice to our spouses. You are saying that even though "I" can do it by myself, "I" am willing to place my "I" into "Unity" so that we can become a "Unit." When we decide to take this Christian walk, we make the choice to lose the "I" so that Christ might live in us. Therefore, not "my" or "I" will, but Thine will be done, on earth as it is in heaven. "Saying, Father, if thou be willing, remove this cup from me: nevertheless not my will, but thine, be done." (Luke 22:42)

We give ourselves, then we join ourselves, in order to promote, uplift, encourage, and grow someone else. At the stage of marriage, we should have grown up, so now it will be our time to help grow someone else. In submission, we present, not bow down. Marriage isn't and will NEVER be a dictatorship. If that is the case, you need to review why you got married. It is not to boss someone else. It is to build up someone else.

3

Women are gentle creatures. We endure so much. Some of us have endured abuse, (both physical and mental), tears, discouragement, unstableness, faults, mental distress, along with so many other feats. Our strength comes from defeating all of that. But women of God, submission has no part in being abused; it does not equal defeat; it does not mean to defend neither your independency nor your individuality. Being submissive will not make you less of a woman, but a greater woman.

We are a world of change, a people of change; therefore, we must learn to adapt. If we all stayed the same, do you know how boring we would be to one another? One's individuality is simply to know who you are, while independency is being who you are on your own. You will never lose those parts of yourself; it will always remain there. Everything that is a part of your individuality-independency, other attributes, characteristics, etc. - has levels of maturity and they are all adaptable. A thing of uniqueness is learning the levels of being an individual of independency. From birth to death, your independency was there. Let's examine....

As one starts off as newborn and infant individuals, they depend on their parents for many things; feeding them, loving them, holding them, comforting them, and clothing them, but yet in some ways babies (individuals) are independent. Babies move their fingers, their head, and their toes by themselves; babies have the nature of sucking by themselves, babies open their eyes by themselves, and they naturally learn how and when to cry along with labeling each cry in order for the parents to understand. But here's a little sidenote; the parents, even as being developed, mature independent individuals, depend on the babies to let them know what exactly they need by the way they cry; wow, a form of submission!

Even as you grow, so does your level of independency. You learn to see for yourself; you learn to tie your own shoes; you learn to dress yourself; even walk by yourself...eventually, you begin to think for yourself, learn life lessons, and make sound decisions. But all those things come with maturity. These things you never, ever lose, so how can you say that you are no longer independent when you become married? Are we not ever learning creatures? Where did it go? It did not leave; all those things just matured to their next level. People can't think for us always; we continue to have choices to make and things that we must deal with. Did you not know that God will not go above your own will? He will not go against your will.

Before we began to walk, we had to learn to crawl; but understand that once we learned to walk, we had no need to crawl any more. Before we began to utter one single syllable, we cried; but once we learned how to fully hold a conversation, we had no need to cry our conversations out all the time. Just because some things that were a part of us being an independent individual dropped off, it will never conclude that we are no longer independent. It matures us for whatever the next level of our life is; this I cannot stress enough.

Here's another sidenote: When we continue to listen to others who don't have a spouse, or others who have been abused by the opposite gender, or those who have hate for other genders, then we have now submitted to the thoughts and feelings of someone else. One thing I have learned is, "Hurt people, hurt people." And we have now allowed those same "hurt" people to inform and tell us how to handle the next step in our lives concerning marriage. We have now allowed someone else to put our life together. Now where is the independency in that? God gave you a mind of your own, along with wisdom and knowledge. And if that is something that you lack, the Bible instructs to ask for it; seek Him for it. "And I say unto you, Ask, and it shall be given you; seek, and ye shall find; knock, and it shall be opened unto you." (Luke 11:9) That way you will never go wrong, and it won't leave you still confused. God is not the author of confusion.

The focus on where our independency lies is very important. Acquiring our heart's desire, gaining prominent careers, and other things as such are part of our independent side, but now in order to move on and upward, we must let those things become a part of our achievement side. Those tangible things will always be a part of me, but they cannot dictate who I am and they won't keep me from my destiny of being united in Holy Matrimony.

One of the beauties of being independent is having the will to do the right thing. Making the right decision and being the boss of your mind is an awesome thing. Have you ever been proud of a decision you recently made? You were proud because it made you feel authoritative in whatever the decision consisted of. How did you feel when you made that first decision to live for Christ? Wonderful, wasn't it? Wow, you made the step to live your life in the maturity and nourishing of Christ. What authority you have!!! Your mind has now become the mind of Christ and what He stands for you will stand for. You presented your life to Christ in order for Him to spiritually review it and line it up with the will of God. Now what would you call this? Yes, that's it...the art of submissiveness!

Did you know that Christ served with a level of submission?

Think About It.....

Ephesians 5:25 says, "Husbands, love your wives, even as Christ also loved the church, and gave himself for it;"

There is another level of a woman's independency that God wants us to learn; Knowing how to love your Head and appreciating him all as a whole...The art of submissiveness.

Ephesians 5:21-22 says, "Submitting yourselves one to another in the fear of God. Wives, submit yourselves unto your own husbands, as unto the Lord."

CHAPTER THREE
The Art of Submissiveness....
Knowing He's Always A-HEAD of You

"Wives, submit yourselves unto your own husbands, as unto the Lord." (Ephesians 5:22)

Ladies, do you know who your Head is: In all matters of life, it is God; in all matters of marriage, it is your husband. God is the Head-leader of all life.

"...before me there was no God formed, neither shall there be after me." (Isaiah 43:10b)

"This people have I formed for myself; they shall shew forth my praise." (Isaiah 43:21)

"Thou shalt have no other gods before me." (Exodus 20:3)

He created the earth and the fullness thereof and all the life that exists within it. "The earth is the LORD'S, and the fulness thereof; the world, and they that dwell therein." (Psalm 24:1) He is the only true and living God, wise, and His knowledge has no end.

One important thing that the Bible teaches us is...

"For my thoughts are not your thoughts, neither are your ways my ways, saith the LORD. For as the heavens are higher than the earth, so are my ways higher than your ways, and my thoughts than your thoughts." (Isaiah 55:8-9)

You cannot assume the ways or thoughts of the Head. Those thoughts can only be revealed. They can't be seen with the naked eye. That same authority has been inherited and given to man...

"But I would have you know, that the head of every man is Christ; and the head of the woman is the man; and the head of Christ is God." (1 Corinthians 11:3)

For God created man and He created woman from man. Sorry, ladies, you can't take credit for something that you didn't create.

The Bible speaks...."For the man is not of the woman; but the woman of the man. Neither was the man created for the woman; but the woman for the man." 1 Corinthians 11:8-9.

We were created for the need of being a helpmeet; the cure for man's loneliness. "And the LORD God said, It is not good that the man should be alone; I will make him an help meet for him." (Genesis 2:18)

I remember hearing my pastor speak about his level of ministry. He started off by talking about how early the Lord began to deal with him. Sometimes he would wake up at 5:00 am or maybe even earlier than that; perhaps 3:00 am or 4:00 am. While our regular day may begin at 7 or 8 o'clock in the morning, his day would have already started. When we wake to commune with God, the doors of God's church opened way before we even thought or dreamed about waking up. My pastor would have already prayed for our dreams, our ministries, our circumstances, and more. Wherever we are, or whatever the need may have been, he had already prayed for it. I'll never be able to fathom where his mind is. He is A-HEAD of us.

First, just because he is our shepherd and being assigned to our spiritual life, gives him that Head authority. Shall we say that it makes him A-HEAD of us? Second, him having early fellowship with God keeps him always AHEAD of us.

This is true of our spouses as well. They have the authoritative charge to be deal with situations way before we could ever come up with any solution. There are many things that he has foreseen and will see through his Godly fellowship.

"Therefore as the church is subject unto Christ, so let the wives be to their own husbands in every thing." (Ephesians 5:24)

There were many times that my husband had a Godly solution to a problem that I didn't know existed, but he knew it would happen. It just made me say, WOW! He may not have ever been in the situation before, but his authority of being my head kept me from being in a world of trouble. Just having a civil conversation with him keeps me in awe of him because he is two years younger than I and yet his level of maturity is amazing. Some things were taught to him as a child but as he continued throughout life, he learned on his own. His knowledge of life is wonderful, and I figured out a long time ago that I needed his leadership on various areas of this marriage and my individual life. His strength has made me strong in my weakness. That makes him always A-HEAD of me and our household as well.

If our spouse's thought patterns was on the same level as ours, then why get married? We could do it all by ourselves. I got married because of love and because I realized that I needed him to make my dreams complete. I wasn't afraid to admit that I could not do it by myself. Spouses, being the head of us, bring out some of our best fruits that have yet to be used. Our husbands are also A-HEAD of us because God gave him the authority to be that way. Now all emotions aside, do we really want that kind of authority? Well, speaking from the standpoint of a wife and mother-NO, NO, NO and final answer-NO!!! But let me make it absolutely clear, I'm here to help, not hinder his calling. We as married women of God need to allow our husbands to always stay A-HEAD of us. That does not mean we are inferior to him or fearful of being ourselves because being ourself is one of many things that caught the attention of our spouse. It was because of our submissive relationship with God that caused him to want to get to know that wonderfully and fearfully made person you are today. He knew he needed someone that wouldn't hinder God from always making him A-HEAD.

Women of God, beauty lies in our obedience. There are blessings in being obedient. This holds true in every aspect of life where leadership is evident. From your leader at work, to your leader at home, we owe it to ourselves to be blessed, but it comes through our obedience to those who are A-HEAD of us. We shouldn't let our pride and emotional beings get in the way of allowing God to truly mold us and shape us into being who He meant us to be. Approach is very important. We have to get it in our minds, which should be the mind of Christ, to let God be God and allow those whom He has given to us to be our heads to truly be our heads. Fret not ladies, we are still somebody in the eyes of the Lord. We're even a stronger example to the world when we do things God's way.

CHAPTER FOUR
At What Point Do We Become One?

Now, if he's always A-HEAD of us, then at what point do we become one? Well, for starters, God's union allows married couples to become one in flesh.

"And said, For this cause shall a man leave father and mother, and shall cleave to his wife: and they twain shall be one flesh? Wherefore they are no more twain, but one flesh. What therefore God hath joined together, let not man put asunder." (Matthew 19:5-6)

We are one in spirit because we are equally yoked. Serving the same God, believing the same Word, and being filled with the Holy Ghost brings forth the livelihood of unity within a marriage. Having natural things in common works as well, but not having the love of God in the same way, that's worth nothing. Any small defect will allow the enemy space to cause a continuation of disruption. We leave our security blankets (dependency) of home and cleave to one another. "Therefore shall a man leave his father and his mother, and shall cleave unto his wife: and they shall be one flesh." (Genesis 2:24) That becomes our new level of unity. You wouldn't believe the numerous things James (my husband) and I have in common just because we are saved, sanctified, and filled with the Holy Ghost. We love God, we love church, we love God's music, we love the Word of God, and we love souls.

This allows our thought patterns to be one. They (our thoughts) are all aligned with the will of God. We are finding out that what pleases God pleases us always.

Our oneness also includes our goals in life. In the natural sense we are always seeking out financial and educational plans. The things that we have the desire to do, we want to do them together in harmony so that it will flow better. When no oneness is there, it could destroy the will of God because of one person's personal agenda, causing the unity of marriage to be broken.

I remember when the conversation of selling financial securities came up. My first reaction and thought to the whole idea was absolutely not! My emotional thinking process went through the roof. "It'll never work, everybody's doing it, there is no security in it, it's a pyramid scam, we can't afford to do it right now..." All of those negative thoughts went on and on from my lips of clay (you know, those same lips I used to utter to the Lord to shape, mold, and make in His image). My goal went from supporting him to trying to make him abort the whole idea of pursuing it. Oh, our goals were the same, but when the opportunity came, it was from a source that I didn't trust enough, so the unity was broken. Instead of me allowing James to always be A-HEAD of the situation, I wanted to be ahead of him. I just knew that my idea was right. Well, sorry again, I was wrong, dead wrong.

My mind was not as open as his, and if his mind would have closed as well, we would be out of business and out of the will of God. That's just one example. I said all of that to say that though you are one in many areas, you still must allow your spouse to always stay A-HEAD, because it is his responsibility to know what God feels is best for the marriage. Pretending to be strong and actually being strong are totally different things. If you didn't realize that a car had the right of way, meaning you didn't let it go ahead of you, then you would crash right into it. Your dreams are his dreams and his desires are your desires; what concerns you concerns him and vice versa. What's different though is the method of producing those things that are in your heart and mind that you desire to become a reality.

While our enthusiasm might speak to go for it as soon as possible, the spouse might foresee warning signs and will ask that we do some special preparation for that possibility. The Bible even lets us know to be anxious for nothing. "Be careful for nothing; but in every thing by prayer and supplication with thanksgiving let your requests be made known unto God." (Philippians 4:6) What is there may seem good but could also be a mirage. We must learn to see the whole truth and the spirit behind that truth. It's meant for husbands to see those things. It's meant for wives to understand those things that he has seen. Oneness simply means unity which can also be identified as solidarity. Still wondering at what point you become one? Well, it's at the point where oneness exudes peace, because when there is peace, then it allows camaraderie to be effective in one's marriage. Learning to subconsciously stay in our lane while we are pursuing the same goal as our husband's goal is a marvelous thing. There is no oneness in competition, but in completion.

CHAPTER FIVE
Where Do We Go From Here?

"Let the husband render unto the wife due benevolence: and likewise also the wife unto the husband." (1 Corinthians 7:3)

Well, where exactly do you want to go from here? I will leave this section open for you to write down and speak out your future plans in your marriage. Just use Godliness and maturity. You can reference the previous chapters in this book to assist you.

I want you and your husband to use the remaining assigned pages to write out where you really desire things to go from this point on in your life to have a healthy marriage that you and God will be pleased with. Talk it out with your spouse. Make it a fun experience, but be as truthful and as transparent as can be. Show the world what Godly agape (unconditional) love looks like. Remember, this is all about oneness and teamwork, so both parties must participate and work together. It's understandable that marriages do become stagnant, but in the Word of God it says, "The steps of a good man are ordered by the LORD: and he delighteth in his way." (Psalm 37:23) and "The thief cometh not, but for to steal, and to kill, and to destroy: I am come that they might have life, and that they might have it more abundantly." (John10:10)

In the chapters of this book, you have read what marriage could and should be from the perspective of the Word of God and my humble opinion. As women, we are afraid sometimes to allow our husbands to shift gears, so we consciously and unconsciously encourage them to stay in park with something as simple as a funny look because we are too stubborn to become neutral while our husbands drive as we ride comfortably in the passenger seat of our marriage as we go on a journey to the next level. I'm not ashamed to admit that I am often times stubborn. I am also not afraid to admit that I do still have some growing to do. It's now up to you and I, Women of God!!!

IN CONCLUSION...

At the end of the day, to know that at least one goal has been completed is such an accomplishment. I use that same scenario with my marriage. Each day, I set forth the goal to see a smile on my husband James' face. I look forward to overcoming the challenges that have been set before me as an individual and as my husband and I being one in our marriage. Every day is not easy and some days are just downright hard to deal with. With the guidance of God, the power of the Holy Ghost, the leadership of my husband, and the vessel of myself, Mrs. Dianna Bethany, I will overcome and conquer. Step by step and day by day, be encouraged!

God bless you!

Evangelist and Psalmist Dianna Bethany

"Wherefore they are no more twain, but one flesh. What therefore God hath joined together, let not man put asunder."

Matthew 19:6

Husband's or Wife's Thoughts...

"Marriage is honourable in all, and the bed undefiled: but whoremongers and adulterers God will judge."

Hebrews 13:4

Husband's or Wife's Thoughts...

> "Let this mind be in you, which was also in Christ Jesus."
>
> Philippians 2:5

Husband's or Wife's Thoughts...

"Husbands, love your wives, even as Christ also loved the church, and gave himself for it;"

Ephesians 5:25

Husband's or Wife's Thoughts...

"For the husband is the head of the wife, even as Christ is the head of the church: and he is the savior of the body."

Ephesians 5:23

Husband's or Wife's Thoughts...

"Submitting yourselves one to another in the fear of God."

Ephesians 5:21

Husband's or Wife's Thoughts...

"Wives, submit yourselves unto your own husbands, as unto the Lord."

Ephesians 5:22

Husband's or Wife's Thoughts...

"But I would have you know, that the head of every man is Christ; and the head of the woman is the man; and the head of Christ is God."

1 Corinthians 11:3

Husband's or Wife's Thoughts...

"For the man is not of the woman; but the woman of the man. Neither was the man created for the woman; but the woman for the man."

1 Corinthians 11:8-9

Husband's or Wife's Thoughts...

> "And the LORD God said, It is not good that the man should be alone; I will make him an help meet for him."

Genesis 2:18

Husband's or Wife's Thoughts...

"Therefore as the church is subject unto Christ, so let the wives be to their own husbands in every thing."

Ephesians 5:24

Husband's or Wife's Thoughts...

"And said, For this cause shall a man leave father and mother, and shall cleave to his wife: and they twain shall be one flesh?"

Matthew 19:5

Husband's or Wife's Thoughts...

"Wherefore they are no more twain, but one flesh. What therefore God hath joined together, let not man put asunder."

Matthew 19:6

Husband's or Wife's Thoughts...

"Therefore shall a man leave his father and his mother, and shall cleave unto his wife: and they shall be one flesh."

Genesis 2:24

Husband's or Wife's Thoughts...

"Let the husband render unto the wife due benevolence: and likewise also the wife unto the husband."

1 Corinthians 7:3

Husband's or Wife's Thoughts...

"The steps of a good man are ordered by the LORD: and he delighteth in his way."

Psalm 37:23

Husband's or Wife's Thoughts...

"Nevertheless let every one of you in particular so love his wife even as himself; and the wife see that she reverence her husband."

Ephesians 5:33

Husband's or Wife's Thoughts...

"A virtuous woman is a crown to her husband:"

Proverbs 12:4a

Husband's or Wife's Thoughts...

"Whoso findeth a wife findeth a good thing, and obtaineth favour of the LORD."

Proverbs 18:22

Husband's or Wife's Thoughts...

"So ought men to love their wives as their own bodies. He that loveth his wife loveth himself."

Ephesians 5:28

Husband's or Wife's Thoughts...

"But if any man love God, the same is known of him."

1 Corinthians 8:3

Husband's or Wife's Thoughts...

"And we know that all things work together for good to them that love God, to them who are the called according to his purpose."

Romans 8:28

Husband's or Wife's Thoughts...

"According as he hath chosen us in him before the foundation of the world, that we should be holy and without blame before him in love:"

Ephesians 1:4

Husband's or Wife's Thoughts...

"And to know the love of Christ, which passeth knowledge, that ye might be filled with all the fulness of God."

Ephesians 3:19

Husband's or Wife's Thoughts...

"And we have known and believed the love that God hath to us. God is love; and he that dwelleth in love dwelleth in God, and God in him."

1 John 4:16

Husband's or Wife's Thoughts...

"We love him, because he first loved us."

1 John 4:19

Husband's or Wife's Thoughts...

Loving memories and still going strong!

forWord
BOOKS

John 1:1 In the beginning was the Word...

CONTACT US VIA EMAIL AT FORWORDBOOKS@GMAIL.COM

Made in the USA
Las Vegas, NV
30 September 2023